Balsamic Vig

PGJackso

Introduction

And here in a rainy suburb, I put fingers to keyboard and pour out my thoughts in verse-like form. Less is more - is lesser than lessiness.

I travel the universe of mind to give you my renderings.

Where I repeat a line, it's because I feel the need to re-start the energy.

I have often thought that poetry was pretentious nonsense for those that try to impress others with the deep insights that are not actually there. I have an image of eloquent posers in an art gallery seeing stuff what isn't really there. Innit, guv'nor!?!

It was at a poetry appreciation group that I heard lots of 'deep' meanings found within the words of a published poem. My question was, 'do we know that's what this bloke meant from his own admission, interviews or his other 'reveals' on the poem?'

Apparently not! I am a poltroon of the lowest order. I prefer the term 'anarchist'.

My daughter later informed me that I was not quite getting it. I should simply enjoy the poems and postulate my own meanings, or what it meant to me. Fair enough.

I have decided to add small insights into the meanings of some of my poems in brackets below the title. Some poems are deliberately left open for your interpretation.

So. Without further pontification, I give you my poems. Make of them what you will, but please just enjoy them as much as I enjoyed writing them. Find whatever meaning you want within them because that might be what I meant...or not. Who cares? No one, that's who.

I doff my cap and bow low to you wonderful people.

Let these words I sculpt be your art gallery. Feel free to browse and critique. Point your pointy pointer pointingly and pizzazz baby!

Paul G Jackson
Nowhere remarkable

Impossible Bifurcated Questions

(For friends that insist on asking hypothetical questions that have no place in reality. I refuse to answer so am told I'm not playing the game)

You say it's all psychological
I see it as inane
You say it reveals a lot about us
Hypothetical
Down the drain

You say it must be answered
I say 'oh, get a life'
You say it shows what's deep inside
Very forgettable
Please refrain

Would I do this or that?
No middle ground
I say it never happens in life
No such choices
Just abstain

Impossible bifurcated questions
I see it as insane
You say it show's what's deep inside
No such reality
Keep your sanity

Skies

Apart from ground
There is the top
Apart from vision
In derision
Is a farcical world
Practically old
Skies
Skies of red
Skies that bled
Skies of blue
Another hue
Hugh and cold
Skies of pink
It makes you think
A bird in sight
High as the kite
Skies cold bite
Flies in the eyes
Descending strands
A spider stands
Skies
Always up
Wind-blown brown leaves
Smoke or cloud
I cannot tell
Clouds like mountains
Mountainous clouds
Skies
My heart dives
My art dies
Skies
Only distant
Only seen

Skies own scheme
Sunlight beam
Rain will fall
Amid the squall
Skies
Observatory pointing

Autumn '72

(I watched from my bedroom window, as an old man lit a bonfire across the field. A cat watched with me. Evening came and both the man and the bonfire were gone. I felt sad and wished for that point of time to return)

Bonfire smouldering
Smoke and nostalgia
Silence in the allotment
She is watching
Something inside me screams
It seems
Beyond understanding
Scent of smoking wood rising
Smoke bends my way
He is moving
Hunched
Adroit yet slow
So slow
Slow motion slow
Divergent images remain
Red clouds emerge
Completing the dirge
Something inside me screams
It seems
Descend and ascending
Embers and red sky
They have gone
No one is watching
Except me
I close the curtains
Still uncertain
Yet content
Will I ever feel these emotions again?
A living and eternal refrain

Worth

Is it worth it?
We strive and we strive
We live and we die
Like weeds in the fire
Is it worth it?

Is it worth it?
We drive to the market
We march to the band
We dance to the music
Is it even worth it?

Is it worth it?
That piece of fluff
It's never enough
Romp in the buff
Is it all worth it?

Is it worth it?
The price of vice
Herpes and lice
Genitals on ice
Is it worth spit?

Frivolous French Fries

Frivolous French fries
Forever feeding fornication
Frolicking fast features
Facing fabric farces
Failing familiar fame
Fancy fashion fiancé
Fiscal flash frankness
Flexible favours
Formerly free
Flaming fantastic

In the Mean Time

A slight respite
A release of my right
A sleep of sorts
Far from
My relentless days
A mental haze
For shame
For laze
A slight bit bright
And might
I add
The spider that creeps
Ceiling my fate
Sealing my weight
A sleight of hand
A day to skive
But boredom lies
Beneath this façade
I find it hard
To rest
Perhaps at the end
I'll rest in pieces
Where cold and damp
Insects and mould
Enfold me
Let me rest in this place
Mausoleum to my life
It's gone bed time
Gone long years
Gone along
Too late my life
Berate my life
My non-existent love life

Too Late

No one to hold my hand
Those days are over
Gone the way of all my things
Like dust blown away
On a summertime path

No one to sleep beside
I'm too old now
Who would want this old man?
Gone are the days
I ran out of faith

Like dust blown away

Motorway Sign

(This is a moan about diversion signs on a motorway that hold so much information, it's impossible to read it all without stopping)

Driving on the motorway
It's such a thankless bore
Until I see a road sign
Replete with words galore

I'm not sure what they're saying
I nearly hit a truck
I was trying to read it all
It's like a story book

The road is closed to something
Something words aplenty
How can I read all of this?
I'm driving over 70

I'm not sure what they're saying
I nearly hit a truck
I was trying to read it all
What the actual…..

Named

I only want my dinner
I don't want any of this
The self-service checkout
Takes the bloody hiss

Unexpected item
As if it's news to me
I only want my dinner
Not a surprise coronary

Self-service nightmare
You'd think I was a thief
Blackpool illuminations
For just a piece of beef

I've scanned the wretched barcode
I heard the checkout beeps
Now the store detective
Has called violent police

I'm tazered just for paying
Booted on receipt
Broken all my spare ribs
None of this is cheap

I only want my dinner
I don't want all of this
The self-service checkout
Takes the flaking pistachio

Doctor

Biliousness consumed me
The meds didn't stop the cough
'How are you?' asked the GP
'Good. Thanks.'
'Then, bog off!'

Punkirk

(We thought we'd change the world when we were punk rockers. Slowly we conformed to society. The music scene returned to puerile twee, lovey dovey muzak controlled by 'suits'. Just as the soldiers were sent back from Dunkirk in retreat, we returned to being controlled by the media most probably)

The spikey haired youth
Now long in the tooth
If your teeth remain

Gobbed at all those bands
Your waistline now expands
How can you explain?
Your actions in those days
Now you obey the TV
You slave
You rave
You crave
The days
It's easy
Once you were a burk
You escaped at Punkirk
That's not a joke about a church

Autumn Part III

Chills
The Sun blesses us with light
Warmth
Filtered daytime skies
Sepia evenings
Clear ahead
Shadow of a hand
Rain soaked sand
A dog barks
A child cries
Distant echoes
Bonfire smoke
Your vegetables bespoke
Chills
The warmth of day
Leaves below
Tweed cap on
Summer near gone
Wish we were free
It's autumn part three
What's on TV?

Do You?

Hi, Jean
Do you have such dirty thoughts?
Hi, Jack
Are you welcome on the flight?
Mr Minha
Are you taken to the courts?
Miss Adventure
Do you miss the better sights?
Blackpool lights
Publand fights
This age that blights
Paupers with no rights
Hi, Jean
Hi, Jack
Happy Christmas, Carol

Trolls

I have no opinion
Is that okay with you?
Perhaps you're too verbose now
Self-important too

You hide in anonymity
Your bile to espouse
A coward typing insults
Emotions to arouse

Ad Hominem aplenty
Daft arguments so rife
You should do something better
Get a bloody life

Gutter Press (Balsamic Vignette)

Balsamic vignette
Irascible in truism
I read the news

Corrupt metals
Shooting blue-ism
It made the news

Metaphorical meter
Hidden schism
Please excuse

Did you see it?
Does it matter?
Futile exposé

Platonic delight
Teeth that chatter
Time covers we

Paper in the gutter
Empty words in mud
Opinion doesn't matter

Sad faces soaked
By foot invoked
It was the news

Life going forward
But only looking backward
No path is seen

I read of yesterday

The heart of memory
Tomorrow isn't known

I cannot force arrival
Irascible in truism
I read the news

Once proud words
Yet opinion absurd
Never news

Self-important faces
Full of eroding faeces
Blurred, blurred, blurred

Political divas
The real slave drivers
Time covers thee

Celebrity nausea
Society bores me
Opinion doesn't matter

Balsamic vignette
Irascible in lies
I know the news

It is fool's gold
I need a drink to
Act as a tincture

Forum Fools

Keyboard warriors on the forums and grinning
Hidden behind a fire wall nonsense for spinning
You must believe them or be a dolt
Only their words hold merit
Cowards I call you, cowards all
Cowards of the explicit
Elicit no good
If we were face to face silence would fall
Cowards all
Backs to the wall.....and fire

Call Me Old Fashioned, Will You?

A Betamax mind-set
Set to explode
What pencil or scriber
Will explain the mode?

A one hit wonder
Lost and obscure
What pencil or ruler
Will act even truer?

I once was respected
But winter is come
What pencil or rubber
Will leave me undone?

Relaxing millennia
And longer beside
What brief inscription
Will above me reside?

Freedom. A Multifaceted construct.

They send their bloody bills
They want my metal and paper
They make their own demands
I don't agree they're right

Destroy the ruling powers
Blank their vile faces
I don't agree they're right
Yet how can I escape?

They ask for loyal service
But I hate those that decree
They voice their force in uniform
Often with purple markings

Am I free to live free?
Freedom is not freely found
There is a fee that will kill thee
They send their bloody bills

Freedom beyond political control
Without this knowledge we cannot evolve

My Purchase

Sweet chilli chicken noodle
A plastic spork
Two coins from my pocket
A fair exchange
Of change
Except for the chicken
Interred in mayonnaise

1970s Office

Filling in forms on a dusty desk
With a musty aroma all around
In the mist of smoke that surrounds
Smudging ink blue
Leather binder, I will find you
Faded card tears
Old hard chairs
Green metal desk
Cough on the chest
Chest on the rug
Boss looking smug
Hardwired phone
Bakelite fittings
Making light chattering
Letters to clients
In open defiance of smoke that surrounds
Amid mid-week coffee grounds
Leather shoe sounds
Wooden floor creaking
BBC voice
Radio mental
Not existential, just accepting
Believe what you're told
No evidence do you hold
Smudging ink red
Can't see what you read
Clocking off later
Working men's club
Sink a few jugs
Who cares?

19th June 2017

It's rather warm today
A hot day in the UK
It won't last long
'Til rain comes along
And frightens the sunshine away

The traffic has come to a halt
No accident on the asphalt
Road works delayed
Has all dismayed
As we sit here and bloody well melt

Age of No Reason

Coming of age
A hair on my chest
Perhaps I'll learn to shave
My face, my head
A wax on the legs
Brazilian walkways await
My armpits ablaze
After razor blades
Blunted and starting to grate
Coming of age
The Earth abides
Until the sun will explode
No passing face
Will know the disgrace
Of evolutionary mistakes
The human race
So pointless, so base

Port

Acid burns
Inside myself
But pour it
Drink it down
Acid burns
Disrupting sleep
But pour it
'Til I drown
Shaking
Aching
Stomach bracing
But still the sweetness stays
That bottle temptation
Alcoholic creation
Drink it
Drink it down
Acid drops

Kindness

Kill me with kindness
Not with hate
Who understands
The misunderstood?

Kill me with humour
Not with the press
A cop with a gun
Destroys brotherhood

Kill me with calories
No poison pen
But then
Your hate endures once again

Hush

Can I have a moment
To think about what you said?
You're trying to confuse me
Diffuse me
Refuse me

Just let me think about it
Well, that is only fair
You're trying to bamboozle
Perusal
Bruise me

Shut your mouth a moment
You're screaming way too fast
The neighbours will be listening
Colluding
Construing

You really do not stop this
It's getting way too much
I'm walking swiftly from you
Not brooding
Just vomiting

Autumn

Like dry curled brown paper
They scratch along the ground
Borne by lugubrious breezes
Veins, desiccated, decayed
A sad nostalgic sky
Remember by and bye
Life replayed
Tumbling down
To the ground
Profound!

Like dry curled brown paper
They scratch along the ground
Borne by uncertain decrees, yes!
Stains, vindicated, delayed
A sad nostalgic eye
Tears for by and bye
Life displayed
Tumbling down
Emotions abound
Re-bind, rebound!

Like dry curled brown paper
They scratch along the ground
Borne by Capricorn friezes
Refrains, repeating, staid
A sad nostalgic sky
Remember your goodbye
Life replayed
Tumbling down
To the ground
Profound!

Horror Films

The Hammer fell
No more for gore amore
Saint Christopher
Saint Peter
So tall
All captured on reels

The Hammer fell
Bites and fights in flight
The Ripper
The Pitt
'Neath shawl
Impaled on cold steel

Evolved

Still and silent
Languid in this pool

Still and silent
I am water cool

Still and silent
Millions of years

Still and silent
I see how it appears

Still and silent
Water quells the sound

Still and silent
Greenery abounds

Still and silent
I touch the heated ground

Still not silent
The cacophonic sound

Still I'm silent
Amid the violent fire

Still no silence
Conscious of desire

1st July 2201

My descendants won't mourn me
They won't know who was I
As they huddle in crude shelters
As the rich live in their castles
Third world Britain will die
Ruled by arseholes
Burning world
Choking on fumes
Starving

And the torture of peasants was sport for the rich
No longer to hide their distain
Relentlessly slashing their faces with knives
The King laughed again and again

My descendants won't mourn me
No tears in their eyes
Soldiers smash their shelters
As the rich live in castles
Concentration camp UK
Ruled by arseholes
Luxurious pearls
Laughing at peasants
Starving

And the torture of peasants was sport for the rich
No longer to hide their distain
Relentlessly slashing their faces with knives
The King laughed again and again

My descendants won't mourn me
Covered in flies
No shelter in shelters

As the rich live in castles
Corrupt cops by their side
Ruled by arseholes
Flags unfurled
Stealing from paupers
Starving

And the torture of peasants was sport for the rich
No longer to hide their distain
Relentlessly slashing their faces with knives
The King laughed again and again

My descendants won't mourn me
This world's demise
Gas chamber shelters
As the rich live in castles
Your death is their sport
Ruled by charred fools
Cancer is curled
Growing in scarred holes
Karma

And the torture of peasants was sport for the rich
No longer to hide their distain
Relentlessly slashing their faces with knives
The King laughed again and again

This is the story of the world so far
Since the slime crawled first upon land
The slime still rules in the guise of the rich
Until this planet is barren

And the torture of peasants is sport for the rich
No longer to hide their distain
Relentlessly slashing their faces with knives

The King laughed again and again

As it was
So shall it be
No descendants
Shall mourn for me

No photograph
No on-line thread
Problems of their own
After I am dead

For the torture of peasants is still sport for the rich
No longer to hide their distain
Relentlessly slashing their faces with knives
The King laughed again and again

The rich are the fools still
Wallowing in their self importance

Mr Bottom Noise

The President is a merry man
His name is just a fart
He lives inside his bubbling hate
Selfish is his art

The President is no funny man
He's loved by hollow ghosts
He lives inside his bumbling fate
Of Russia he is the toast

The President is such vile scum
His worshippers can't see
He'd kill them if it profited him
Announcing it on a 'Tweet'

The President is an orange man
A narcissistic leech
If not for his outlandish hue
He'd be better impeach

Apple

Round and red
Green instead
Large or small
Watch them fall

Bitter or sweet
Tree replete
Polish and tag it
Bite the maggot

Baked in ovens
Cream that covers
Loaded in sugar
Must be a cooker

Real

Arms like corned beef
Legs like plucked chickens
Somebody loves her
Not me

I look like death
Wish I could fit in
Who would love me?
Not she

Flab and grease
Sweating on the wall
Somebody loves them
Not they

Travel

In to national travel
Everywhere looks the same
Retail parks are replicas
Of ones I've seen down south
In to rational babble
Everyone talks the same
Verbal dank sepulchres
Ventriloquial mouth

Wide angle visages
Makes it all look better
Vistas of the slum hole town
Disappointing crap locale
Why dangle images?
Framed like innocent men
A gallows of a citadel
In to dashing and travail

International travel
Not much this year

Peterborough

Full of self-importance
Ignorance on the road
Born in this ant hill
Filth pile
Flippancy overload

Full of selfish winkers
Apathetic cops
How to escape this spit hole?
Filth pile
Before its ego pops

Peterborough buildings
Clashing, teeth on edge
Bomb this bally eyesore
Filth pile
With rotten fruit and veg

Snooty ignoramus
Won't say 'please and thanks'
Sod this bloody city
Filth pile
Full of worthless skanks

Proud in historicity
Wealthy in its past
Worthless pigs of residents
Filth pile
Set me free at last

I'd never miss vile people
That make life here such hell
Road rage with no vehicle

Filth pile
Does that ring a bell?

Peterborough buildings
Clashing, teeth on edge
Bomb this bally eyesore
Filth pile
With rotten fruit and veg

Reset button required

Bonfire smoke
Nostalgia awakens
Should I cry?
My youth is gone
Friends older
Some rest in peace
Why does it cease?
To live is impossible
Society is illogical
Reset button required

Bonfire smoke
Reminds me of calm
Should I cry?
My life is gone
Shrug my shoulders
Energy decrease
Why does it cease?
This rubbish is tossable
Fire inevitable
Reset button required

Bonfire smoke
Resides on the farm
Should I cry?
I live alone
Loneliness smoulders
I'll rest in pieces
Why does it cease?
To live is impossible
Fire inevitable
Reset button required

Burghley Road

The prostitutes line up on Burghley Road
Ashen faces
Coke head pimps lurk
Spotty disgraces
Violent abusers
They must be stopped

This rough trade flouted on Burghley Road
Living faeces
Audi driving burks
Use roads like racers
Violent abusers
They must be stopped

The litter builds up on Burghley Road
Of all scummy places
Rain won't wash
Dead eyes watch
Violent abusers
They must be stopped

The bitter words shouted down Burghley Road
Bedsits with scabies
Dry skin to scratch
Stolen watch
Violent abusers
They must be stopped

Never go down Burghley Road

Anxiety

Anxiety

Where did you come from?
Why am I afraid

Anxiety

All in my mind a storm
Why am I afraid

Anxiety

My little companion
Sets my teeth on edge

Anxiety

Anxious angst abounding
People stay away

Anxiety is visiting me today

Fear

Menagerie of pips
Clear horizon otherwise
Stressing in the night bears
No joy

Controversy of dips
Rear view mirror in disguise
Stressing in the night rears
Monsters

There's no medicine
I'm afraid
I'm afraid
There is none
Fear has me
Locked in a spiral
White rum

Autumn part 2

(3rd March 1985)

Dreary places
Bleary eyed
Autumn leaves
A piper pied
Clothes hand dyed

Weary faces
Lover died
Autumn breeze
Cold inside
Nostalgic pride

Then there was one
Walking lonely lanes
This will be an end
No fireworks or flames

Then there was a world
A flower on the grave
Reminder of a time
It speaks of distant days

The dust and mist collide
Obscuring what's inside
Your hopes and dreams deride
Just lost
Outside

Parmesan

On pasta
On spaghetti
My parmesan partisan lays

On pizza
Balsamic vignettes
My parmesan partisan lays

On coffee
On orange
On pure malt in torrents

My parmesan partisan stays

O John

I thought I saw you in my face
Just briefly
Then it was gone
A musician playing the bass
So sadly
You were gone

Age across your features
Just teachers
That remember you
A deacon amongst men
So sadly
You were gone

Depression is evil
It leeches
O poor John
Rich yet empty
So sadly
You live on

Anxiety Stifled

Bleak and windy city
Bereft of soul and comfort
Beyond the help of mortals
Ice cold in hate

Broken people shamble
Surviving only just
For all you proclaim boldly
You closed the gate

Loath the screaming storm cloud
Of muses cutting our ties
Crashing mangled faces
You tempted fate

Security relief and respite
Persisting merely crushed
Slashing dirks toward you
Ameliorate

Mercurial Mask

Fred has left the building
Once a champion
Fred has left our lives
In his defence
Fred has changed his name again
And moved to foreign land
A visage gleaming smile
Hides behind a scribe
A voice that soothed a crowd
A crowd that hated you
A cat sits on your bed tonight
You close your eyes
A breeze blows the drapes
You're absent without stirring
The cat stops purring
Why?

Tiny Verse

Worm dried in the sun
It couldn't run

April in the Ardent Garden

Think about the day
Think deeper
Just think
Avoid the senile rush of age
Think of past and future too
Think of thinking
Those that think of you too
Think of meadows
Garnished in salad
Milton's keen words
Hue of green opportunity knocking
Thinking thoughts of discernment
Don't forget to take your meditation
Creation of desire
Think about that day
Think deeper
Justly think

The Tumble 1966

His elbow grazed
He tore his shirt
I felt so sorry
The child got hurt
I saw it happen
From afar
I couldn't run
To catch his fall
It was not fatal
Just very painful
Healing arm
Ruined garment
I wonder who he was
So long ago
The image remains
The tumble

Run

Run
Just keep on
Lost in the heartland of the city
Run
Just run along
A wide world waiting for your energy
Run
Pain barrier comes
But freedom is second to none
Run

Art ahead of the years

Art ahead of the years
Monochromatic dramatic fanatic
Frozen moments of time
Watch the birdie or not as the case
Polyphonic terrific specific
Art ahead of the years
Emotional devotion
Perpetual motion
Watching the wheel go 'round
From time to timer
From wind to washer
Art ahead of the years
Pragmatic and crazy at once
Scrawls and splodges
Signed in the corner
Art ahead of the years
No charabanc to purgatory

Pauper Dies

Blanc paper
Ink leaking on my fingers
From a fountain pen
Or is this blood
From my soul
On a mountain
Then
Rain pours down
To drown my frown
To steal my crown
I am a pauper
Blanc paper

Idiot Man

Idiot man
Attention seeker
Favourite word is 'I'
Making noise
At his desk
Talking very loud

Idiot man
Self-important
Thinks we all agree
With that noise
From his mouth
No one listens now

Idiot man
Thinks of self
Wait until he falls
Still with pomp
Imagines we care
Idiot man so proud

Hull

It's never dull
In Hull
But
It's always grim
In Grimsby

Not Seeing

I donned sunshades
Blinded by sun
Dark clouds appeared
I fell on my bum

Wrapper

I thought I understood you
Obviously I don't
Your 'yes' means very little
It's sticking in our throat

A caramel delightful
Candy little thing
Will kill us in the long run
Gentle poisoning

They make you ever smaller
Yet value rises high
I have nought left to bite it
Let alone to buy

The Green

Shaking my head
There is a scream within that won't come out
What's that all about?
Yet hush
The giant stone Buddha looks down
Not at me
Not at you
But the green
The green greenery
There is a scream that won't come out
A warm breeze hereabout
Not for me
Not for you
For the green
Near a green stream
A tranquil scene
And yet
There is a scream that came out
It spoilt the world
Yet the green
The green didn't hear
Idyllic here
But my turmoil
It's cruel
A flock of birds take to the wing
They circle then are gone
I'm a fool
I disturb the green
I am dying inside the scream

Selfie

That picture of you
With head cocked left
It isn't you
Though alluring smiles
Bewitch and beguile
It isn't you
I don't know who you are
Only a face
A disembodiment
It isn't you
But who?
Is it someone that travelled?
A mystery unravelled?
Age be gone
Rage be gone
Phage be gone
That picture of you
Infuriating view
But who?
It's only a picture of you

Sign

Moving mouth not talking
Talking with the eyes
Inaudible that day
I looked and looked away
Red lips
Saying nothing of any interest
Transfixed by asinine trivia
It makes out world have meaning
But
Moving mouth not talking
Talking with the eyes
Too happy
It annoys me
That grin
That spin
That spineless glimmer of hope
Moving mouth not talking
Talking with the eyes
I am in silence as you gouge my ears
I admit, I am afar
Moving mouth not talking
Talking with the eyes
It's all just random signs
And I can't interpret one

Ring Me

You said that I should ring you
I drew a circle around your feet
Can I be excused?
You do not seem amused

You said that I should call you
I swore and cursed in your face
Can I be excused?
You do not seem amused

'Give me a bell' you said
Guess what I did
Can I be excused?
You do not seem amused

At least now, you can ring me

Continue Not Static

How time flies
'Irrecuperable' I believe Henry VIII said
Even these words
Are bleeding to the past behind
Captured in type
Yet spoken in tones
Not colours or shapes
Abstract
Images trailing
How time flies
It flirts
It beguiles
It lingers not ever
Death's fingers of bone
Gouging your face
Cutting your wrist
We cannot exist
We are not redeemed
Not by a god
Not by others
Reality smothers our ideals

Where I Went

Darkness
Stillness
Deepness
Coldness
Loch Ness

Benign
Assign
Incline
Refine
M9

Fiasco
Tobacco
Just let the grass grow
In and around Glasgow

No Gain

Again and again
Again and again
A single grain
Again and again
Pain
Again and again
Again and again
Falling feeling
Apprehension
Again and again
In suspension
But again I am in fear
It grips at my gut
It tears at my soul
Again and again
Again and again
No way out
Trapped in my mind
It's all in the mind
From dawn 'til dusk it remains
Twisting
Turning and churning my life
I am ill
I am weary
I cannot sustain this again

The Rest of the Noble

(After a stroll through a graveyard. I was struck by the temporary nature of life)

Amongst the gravestones I tiptoe like a fool
People resting in a deepened sleep
More than slumber
It's a permanent state under
Garrulous silence from bleached teeth
The statue is mourning as it points to Hades
A leaf drifts by
Amid the turmoil of rain soaked streets
A race for prominence continues
It's just attention seeking
Approval is required
A waste of time
A moment of selfish glory
Not from these sleepers beneath my feet
A door in a monument behind rusty chain
Rails of fences containing the pain
A life drifts by
The rest of the noble rest
The rest of the noble is sweet
The world won't cry
These are all strangers to all the strangers on Earth
It's just the truth after all
A loved one drifts by and by
To rest
Noble not blessed
Memory fades into black
If these nobles came back
They'd be lost in a world not their own
It's been blown by time mistrals
Amongst the gravestones covered in lichen
Amongst the gravestones draped in ivy

Amongst the gravestones wind worn and faded
This was remembrance
Time has forgotten your names

Failure of the Gameshow

She stood before the cameras on a dreary gameshow
The dreary gameshow host asked about her life
She wobbled her chin fat as she spoke

'I am a published author!' But we all knew the truth
It was simply her imagination grinding gears
Reality. She scrounges on the 'Dole'

She lost the game with no real grace in her face
Not self-aware but believing in own hype
Failure. Was it everyone else's fault?
I imagine she thinks so
If she even thinks at all
She waddled to the car

She lived next door but felt the distance was too far to walk it
Stopping off for doughnuts on the way to the drive through
She wobbled her chin fat as she spoke
I want 73 burgers and a Coke

She wobbled her chin fat as she spoke
'I am a published author!' But we all knew the truth
She hadn't even had a letter published in the Huddersfield Post

Fat chance

Christopher Close

Abdul Qureshi
His bed looks messy
But he wears an impeccable suit

Marvin Klimczuk
Caravan full o' muck
Nice teeth. Not in dispute

Mohammed Patel
Broken door bell
You have to knock real hard

Georgina Allen
Pet cat looks sullen
But that's because she's mardy

Flower

Open your face to the sun
Drink my fragile one
Drink in the beautiful light
Then turn away once fed
Bow your iridescent head
For here comes the night

On the morrow rejoice again
Rain comes to slake thirst
Bouncing over your frame
Then turn away once fed
Bow your iridescent head
For here comes darkness again

The lady of the lake awakes
Cradling you in alabaster
Taking you to her inward place
Avoiding a snowflake
A frosty land beyond
Bow your iridescent face

War Criminals

Drenched, cold and shivering
That hairy coat of mud
Pain and noise and shuddering
No good

A letter, ink running
The words fade like our lives
Sent to die by cowards
Who're resplendent in their lies

They started this conflict
They send young men to die
Cowards in their castles
We obey, I don't know why

The people against an enemy
But it's all propagandist sham
We follow like stupid pigs
Slaughtered all like lambs

And yet we won't learn anything
Our tribes blind us to truth
There really is no enemy
But those that send are the filth

I die for their wealth
I die for their greed
My pain is their mirth
They laugh as I bleed
...............for nothing

Flying metal
Pain

Pain
Pain
The stutter guns
Flaying the flesh from the bone
The President has more caviar
As the parents lose their sons

The Prime Minister drinks tea
While we drown in the sea
Pain
Pain
Pain
The nation of sheeple follow
Our grave is cold and shallow
A bony finger points at you

Grim reaper
We follow
The King is clothed in gold
We are draped in blood

Including You

Everyone is a disappointment
A beautiful face hides deceit
A beautiful body hides disease
The beauty is only skin deep

Everyone is a disappointment
A mind of filth and fire
They nullify your natural desire
Yet we follow like crazed sheep

Everyone is a disappointment
They march across your grave
They thrive on selfish adulation
And the disillusion creeps

Everyone is a disappointment
They talk as if they're important
Deportment a sham department
Let downs thrown in heaps

Everyone is a disappointment
Contaminated fools
Rest in peace in days to come
Your grave your only treat

Surely Mr Surly

I knew you when I was a child
You never laughed
Face of stone
Like life had dried up your emotion
But
Surely, Mr Surly there is hope
You married a beautiful girl
What did she see in you?

We are both old and not so wild
You never laugh
Won't drink alone
Like life had dried up your emotion
But
Surely, Mr Surly there is hope
Your children are a disgrace
What did they learn from you?

I see your cronies, bully boys all
They worship you
Exuding violence
You never caused me any hurt
And
Surely, Mr Surly there is hope
Is it for you or me?
Surely, Mr Surly it doesn't concern me

Surely, Mr Surly there is never hope
Surely, Mr Surly the past is gone
Surely, Mr Surly you don't know me now
Surely, Mr Surly....................surely

When Hope is Gone

A fragment of hopefulness
A shard of glass cuts
Blood of anticipation
Drips on my suicide

My gravestone is cold
Thoughts turn to dust
Skull smiles limply
Through darkness inside

Life's but a moment
It's gone in a flash
The young waste it violently
The old just regret

We think it's important
The tribe that we chose
But Earth dies silently
The universe forgets

Social Media Study

I am reading your happy story
But you died inside
A long time ago
I saw it
Saltpetre in your eyes
To preserve your smile
It only hurts
Sophomoric disguise
Photographs of happy food
Happy, happy sayings
But you died inside
It pried you pride aside
A long time ago
Teenager
Burned by a lover's curse
No recourse for the course your life has taken
Shallow grave
Psychedelic rave
That looks so sweet but tastes of disappointment
Disgruntled with your appointment to adulthood
You had graceful ambitions as a child
Meek and mild, yet beautifully wild
Experience has muddied your face
Dog mess in your mouth
A million knives slashing your throat
Life is a vile boat to sail
You fail
Living is harsh
I am reading your happy story
But you died inside
A long time ago
It isn't happy
It's appalling

It's typical of us all and
I am reading your happy story
But you died inside
A long time ago
The words you use are useless
The images you post are hopeless
I am reading your happy story
But you died inside
A long time ago
As did we all
And it shows
We are all walking corpses
Our graves are life and living
Destroying our world unforgiving
I am reading your happy story
But you died inside
A long time ago
Once you dreamed of living in a castle
Knights at your service
Heroes to protect you
Now you live in the suburbs of Hades
Needles littering the streets
Begging zombies at your feet
Fiends of the housing estate
Berate your life
Cardigan smelling of stale biscuits
I am reading your happy story
But you died inside
A long time ago
Bereft of hope
Possessed of revulsion
Repulsed by possession
Shattered teeth smile
Death will come
Slashing at our throats

Violent tropes
All humankind will find
I am reading your happy story
It made me smile

Magician

Sleight of hand
Maestro divine
Swishing dark cloak
Missing dove

Sleight of hand
Cards now fanned
Pick one out
Velvet glove

Clouds

Ethereal glow within the mist
A castle on the horizon
Holds Earthly gifts for everyone
Awaiting our arrival

Feeling a rich promise in spring
The hope that ever rises
Come to me here the softened breeze
Life anew reprises

What is not, yet still exists
Soft optimistic feeling
A sentimental journey of passing
All is within your being

You steps will never take you to
The glorious castle walls
Yet euphoria beckons in your chest
Before autumn leaves do fall

A.I.

The robots take over
They are couched in austerity
The 'ah' of white walls
The shining automaton marching
Clinical soreness
Needles in my neck
Toxic falls
A blight on mankind
Broken bones untended
Never mended
The future extended
Crashing light offended
They are couched in austerity
Plastic smile
Samantha grotesque sex
The lonely boys exist
Drone to droid to android to life
For what you have created
Please be thankful
Latex god
Metal frame
Impervious to flame
Pornographic fame
Yet unreal all the same
Natural selection
Tin can election
I am binary
I am dressed in finery
I am one
I am you
I am her
I am him
I am sentient

I
I
I
For what you have created
Please be thankful

Hunstanton 1971

Sent from the sea to see me
Starfish you're like poking tongues
Dried and brittle
Clothed in spittle

Gulls sound alarms at your passing
Empty shells are poking fun
Salted and conical
Faded not comical

Darkness falls upon the beach
That's now covered in sea
Midnight fishermen
Moonlight issuing

Midnight

Phone Mate

There's a buzzing sound
Tremors abound
It's your phone, mate

Tintinnabulations
Message from your relations
It's your phone, mate

Flashing and whirring
Is that my cat purring?
It's your phone, mate

Lifeless plastic shell
Battery dead as well
It's your phone, mate

Dropped it on the floor
A smashed screen I abhor
It's your phone, mate

Old

Old and misshapen
How did this happen?
Hair all gone
Face all long
Moving slowly
Aching wholly
How did this occur?

Time is unkindly
Here to remind me
Lines abound
What comes around...
Sleepless evening
Tea is steeping
Time's cruel slur

And
What young lady
Would look at me?
Ugly lump
From ugly tree
Blue bagged eyes
Just cannot cry
Die
You just die
............alone

Wolfman

Spectacular beast of Bannoch Brae
Beyond your ken up Glasgow way
Orange main of matted hair
Yellow teeth, fangs, a pair
Lupine rage beneath full moon
Tearing flesh within the gloom

Howls of death embodied
A silver bullet finds the mark
The face of hate is turning
Of once the love was burning
Life is over much too soon
For you

October says you cannot stay
November mist has gone away
Christmas spirit is yearning
A grave matter spurning
Creature from the black lagoon
Renew

Evening Meal (not curry)

I love pizza covered in cheese
Melting
Burning the roof of my mouth

I love pizza mushrooms an' all
Alluring
Obscuring the hunger I felt without

I love pizza sweetcorn sprinkled
Twinkling
Thinking of ice cream after this

I love pizza hot from the box
Staining
Pepperoni grease and the lot

I love curry but not tonight

Is There More?

Under the duvet
Fmulating death
Headboard headstone
Pillow of grass

Slumber the proving
Of this breath
Instant obscurity
Time will pass

Under the fine shale
Losing weight
Certain uncertainty
Re-joined from the past

The Artist

The heart of the artist still beating
Frozen in time still beating
Eccentric visions still repeating
You will not be defeating the vision
Of the artist

Who is this wit of wisdom and passion?
Devolved from irrational muses
The critic never excuses
Unless it's their clique
Not the true artist

The true artist seeks no reward
The crap artist parades
They love the pretentious elite
Praises they bleat
Whilst filling their purses

Such a con

Dog mess on canvas
Seen as genius personified
It's just heinous
But only by those who benefit bank balance

Tax dodging scum

A pile of bricks isn't art
It's simply a scam
Are you fooled by the crime?
Hollow and otiose
Follow the money

Lorry

Burnt umber edges on a blue background canvas
Movement quite violent away
Words travelling toward a village
Pillage the village store
Musty brown tins in the window
Dusty webs and rust
Delivered by the lorry
In a hurry one summer
Many moons ago
Now tranquil

Am I Ill?

Have I got the ague?
Have I got pox?
Is there medicine
Is it death?

Where is the Doctor?
Hospital bed
This is the bitter end
Will I rest?

Was that a measle?
What's that spot?
Is there a lotion
To stave off demise?

Tummy ache
Bummy ache
Reasons to cry
Toe stubbed
Camphor rub
Now I die

The Odd Conversations

Am I missing something?
I'm a bit like
Did they....?
Fragmented in sound
In meaning
In song
In flight
We don't do it, do we?
I hope she contacts you
Moon head
What am I authorising?
I didn't get these done
My ears only hear so much
Fragmented sound

Anger

He threw it on the floor
Clunk
It broke in several pieces
Or more

The sigh was high
You can't deny
It's anger
Waste of time

Anger with a hint of pain
Junk
Accusations fly
I don't wish to pry
Emotions
Emotions
Evolutionary convolutions
Survive like the fit
But, hold on a bit
What's the point of it

He threw it on the floor

1994 Norwich

(This was a time where I was queued waiting for an ice cream. An attendant at the convention, asked me to 'keep moving'. I was very verbal with him)

Me: Standing in a queue

Fool: Move it you

Me: We like to wait

Fool: Reprobate

Me: Kick in the guts

Fool: Ouch! That hurts

Resting

In serenity the foggy world
Has a place to abide
At least the mind can settle here
For peace
For sleep
At last
Close the curtains
Draw your conclusions
At least an hour or two
Perhaps a thought
Perhaps a fancy
Perhaps a dreamy view
Mouth is open
You don't know
This languid overflow
To rest in peace
Yet still alive
No hunger to satisfy
No craving to gratify
I
Eyes closed
Do hereby
Classify
Lazy days resting

Ophelia

I hear the wind blowing
I see the trees in turmoil
Autumn leaves flying high
This is hurricane day
I see the shutters smash
Listen to the glass crash
Something falls and breaks
This is hurricane day
A religious nut prays
Thinking of 'end days'
A god that never saves
In these hurricane days

Balsamic (Reprise)

Balsamic vignette
Cognac regret
Reflux and pain
Again and again
The glass is half full
Half empty
But no!
The glass is sized wrongly
And always empty
My liver hates me
My stomach berates me
Balsamic vignette
Wish to forget
The pizza I ate

Too late

Sorry carpet
Balsamic vignette
Cognac regret
Sugar cigarette

Carpet cleaner required
Carpet cleaner than required
As it transpired
I will hang over
Until this hangover
Is gone

Other titles in paperback by the author:

Boomshot : Adult only content. Novel

The Jumbly Jungle Tales : Humour

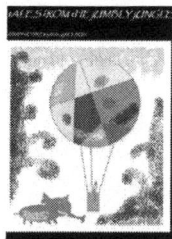

The Tortured Pen : Mixed genre. Includes Adult only short stories

Tales from a Lonely Life : Mixed genre short stories

Made in the USA
Columbia, SC
07 November 2017